Inspirations
FROM THE EVERYDAY

Marilyn,
Be inspired every day!
Tandy

Copyright © 2014 by Tandy Balson
First Edition – July 2014

ISBN
978-1-4602-3612-3 (Hardcover)
978-1-4602-3613-0 (Paperback)
978-1-4602-3614-7 (eBook)

Additional Contributers
Photographer: Ann Edall-Robson
Appears On: Front Cover

Photographer : Tina Fischer
Appears On: Page 1

All rights reserved.

No part of this publication may be reproduced in any form, or by any means, electronic or mechanical, including photocopying, recording, or any information browsing, storage, or retrieval system, without permission in writing from the publisher.

Scripture quotations marked (NLT) are taken from the Holy Bible, New Living Translation, copyright ©1996. Used by permission of Tyndale House Publishers, Inc., Wheaton, Illinois 60189. All rights reserved.

Scripture quotations marked (NIV) are taken from THE HOLY BIBLE, NEW INTERNATIONAL VERSION®, Copyyright © 1973, 1978, 1984 by International Bible Society. Used by permission of Zondervan Publishing House. All rights reserved.

Scripture quotations marked (GWT) are taken from GOD'S WORD, Copyright©1995 by God's Word to the Nations Bible Society. All rights reserved. Used by permission.

Scripture quotations marked (MSG) are taken from THE MESSAGE. Copyright ©1993, 1994, 1995, 1996, 2000, 2001, 2002. Used by permission of NavPress Publishing Group.

Produced by:

FriesenPress
Suite 300 – 852 Fort Street
Victoria, BC, Canada V8W 1H8

www.friesenpress.com

Distributed to the trade by The Ingram Book Company

Tandy Balson sees the world through loving eyes and shares the wonder and awe she sees through her words. In a clear, delicate voice she encourages every heart to open to the gifts in each moment, and to know, no matter how dark and dreary the skies, God is always loving. God is everywhere. In Inspirations from the Everyday, Tandy shares her love and joy and inspires each of us to know and feel and see God's miracles everywhere, everyday.

> Louise Gallagher, Writer. Speaker.
> Author – The Dandelion Spirit.

Beautifully written! Tandy reveals lessons in life's ordinary moments, in a way that is both inspirational, and uplifting. A wonderful book to start each day with!

> Rosemarie McGonigle, Owner/Facilitator
> of Healing Hearts Retreats.

TABLE OF CONTENTS

Dedication	ix
Introduction	xi
Inspirations From Nature	**1**
Snowflakes	3
Melting	4
Snow	5
Adversity	6
Wings Like Eagles	7
Spring Thaw	8
Bumblebees	9
Shelter	10
Heat Wave	11
Geese	12
Echoes	13
Mountain Lakes	14
Seeds	15
Pigeons	16
Off the Beaten Path	17
Autumn Leaves	18
Silence	19
Wings to Fly	20
Inspirations From Around the House	**23**
Recipes	25
Ingredients	26
Broken Dishes	27
Like Silver	28
Photographs	29
Prismatic	30
Recycling	31
Weight Loss	32
Inspirations While Out and About	**33**
Shoulder Rides	35
Don't Rock the Boat	36

Fitting In	38
Carry the Load	39
Crayons	40
Nametags	41
Happiest Place	42
Pool Noodles	43
Not What I Expected	44
Panic Button	45
Duck Races	46
Garage Sales	47

Inspirations From the Seashore — **49**

Abundance	51
As Far As the Eye Can See	52
Broken	53
Diversity	54
Ebb and Flow	55
Erosion	56
Feast or Famine	57
Fishermen	58
Flamingos	59
Footprints in the Sand	60
Garbage or Treasure?	61
Morning's Haze	62
Perseverance	63
Seaweed	64
Sand Bags	66
Thick or Thin	67
Tides	68
Where to Build	69
Winds of Change	70

Inspirations While on the Road — **71**

Rest Area	73
Under Construction	74
Weigh Stations	75
Shadows	76
Hope	77
Life is a Highway – or is it?	78
Recreational Vehicles	79
Are We There Yet?	80
Digital Signs	81

Cruise Control	82
Wait for the Dust to Settle	83

Inspirations From This and That — 85

Donuts	87
Sometimes You Just Need to Show Up	88
Medicine	90
Dance Recitals	91
What Matters Most	92
Big Enough?	93
Surprise!	94
Thanksgiving	96
To or With?	98
Scars	99
Contagious	100
Archery	101
Celebrations	102
A Lesson	103

DEDICATION

This book would not be possible without the ones that I am dedicating it to.

To God, who has given me the gift of finding inspiration in ordinary things. I am blessed beyond belief to be entrusted with this.

To my husband Brian, whose love, support and encouragement has been the wind beneath my wings. Your observations have given me new insights which resulted in several of the stories in this book. Your humour keeps me from taking myself too seriously!

To Ronda Neufeld, who encouraged me to start writing, named my blog, suggested I turn the writings into a book and did the first edit. I can never thank you enough for your belief in me.

INTRODUCTION

The first time I was conscious of God speaking to me through my surroundings was on a beach in Mexico. My husband and I started our days with long walks along a quiet stretch of beach. After a few days I was aware of life lessons being shown to me while we walked. Brian and I talked about these, but I had an overwhelming feeling I was to do more with them. After praying, I felt God telling me to write these lessons down. This was the easy part for me. Far more difficult was when I was directed to share these lessons with others. They felt way too personal to share. When I first found the courage to do so, I was rewarded with positive comments. This made it easier to share again. If you would like to read this, it can be found on my website www.tandyb.com and is titled "Lessons from the Seashore".

Fast-forward a couple of years. A friend encouraged me to start writing on a regular basis and to share these writings on a blog. Although I was very grateful for that first inspiration, I thought it was a one-time thing so resisted the idea. After discussing it with my supportive and encouraging husband, I committed the idea to prayer. The next morning I woke up with the first story in my mind and www.timewithtandy.com was born.

I have been incredibly blessed by the inspirations God has given me through everyday things. My hope and prayer is that you will find something in these writings to inspire, encourage or cause you to look at things in a new way.

♡

Inspirations From Nature

SNOWFLAKES

Our snowflakes are often fine, light and fluffy. Other times they are thick, heavy and wet. Some days they come in both of these plus many forms in between. One day it was even falling in tiny little balls that would have been like hail had they not been so light. I have often heard that no two snowflakes are alike. So far, though, I have been unable to isolate and compare individual flakes to prove this for myself.

A friend shared an amazing photo that she took of a few snowflakes. It showed the intricate and original designs of the individual snowflakes. As I marveled at this photo, I couldn't help but think how each person also has their own original design. Even so-called identical twins have their own unique attributes. No two of us are exactly alike.

Knowing this, why do I still think that others should think or act as I do? I need to remember that God has created each of us with the gifts and abilities needed to serve his purpose for us. He has created us in many shapes and sizes. We are each as unique as snowflakes and each has their own special beauty to share with the world.

For you created my inmost being; you knit me together in my mother's womb. I praise you because I am fearfully and wonderfully made, your works are wonderful, I know full well. Psalm 139:13,14 (NIV)

MELTING

After a week of warm weather, the snow in our yard had melted. There were, however, two small spots where snow remained. This was curious to me. The temperature had been the same in all areas of the yard. Why were there a couple of small areas that hadn't responded the same as the rest did? Upon closer examination, these spots had more shade. They didn't have the advantage of the direct sun. Even the warm temperature could not accomplish what the light of the sun could.

This is also true in life. We may see people whose circumstances seem the same, but some are negative and critical while others are positive and accepting. The change between these attitudes happened for me when I immersed myself in the light of the Son, Jesus. He took my less than favorable circumstances and shone a new light on them to give me hope. When I find myself in the shadows of despair, it's because I have allowed something else to block His light. I have the choice to focus on the small area where the snow remains, or the bigger portion, where the buds of new growth are appearing. I choose to remain in the light of the Son.

May God, the source of hope, fill you with joy and peace through your faith in him. Then you will overflow with hope by the power of the Holy Spirit. Romans 15:13 (GWT)

SNOW

After living in southern Alberta for 7 years, the snow still amazes me. I am originally from Vancouver where the snow comes down in large fluffy flakes that softly float to the ground. It is wet and heavy, and the branches on the evergreens bow under the weight. It piles up quickly but rarely stays for long. When it falls, people panic and their only goal is to get safely home and stay there until the snow is gone. It always amazed me how many people cancelled appointments at just the threat of snow. Snow is not looked on as a thing of beauty, but something to be feared and avoided.

Now, I reside in an area where the snow is small and fine and often blows sideways, seldom just drifting down peacefully. Here it can snow all day and we still don't have much of an accumulation. Driving home one night, I would not have known it was snowing if I hadn't seen it in the headlights of my car. The snow is fine and sparkles like fairy dust. Somehow it seems almost magical. In the morning the appearance of the snow covering the leafless branches of the trees has a beauty that's hard to describe. People here are resigned to the snow, and it doesn't impact their comings and goings. It's something that is expected, but again, not looked on as a thing of beauty.

No matter where I have lived, the children have loved the snow. It's something fun and exciting for them. When I've looked at snow from different perspectives, I realize that it does have some lessons to teach us. You see, in a way we are like snowflakes. Each snowflake is unique, much as people are. On their own they can be quite fragile. When they stick together they can become a force strong enough to stop traffic! While there are many things that one person cannot accomplish, when we band together, we too, can become unstoppable.

How good and pleasant it is when God's people live together in unity!
Psalm 133:1 (NIV)

ADVERSITY

I saw a plant growing on a sandy slope. The solid ground under it had been washed away. What struck me was that not only was it surviving, it appeared to be thriving. There were plenty of leaves and there was evidence of new growth. Others nearby were withering away in the same conditions.

There are times in life when I face the same kind of challenges as this plant. Something happens and I find that the solid ground beneath me has slipped away. The support that I counted on is no longer there. What do I do? How can I carry on? There are times in life when I face situations that are totally beyond my ability to handle.

The good news is that when I cry out to Jesus, He becomes my foundation, my solid ground. When I trust in Jesus, the fear of my circumstances fades and I experience new growth opportunities. It is possible to flourish in the face of adversity, but only if I do not attempt to do it in my own strength. When I surrender to Him, I will not only survive but thrive.

Let us hold unswervingly to the hope we profess, for he who promised is faithful. Hebrews 10:23 (NIV)

Therefore we do not lose heart. Though outwardly we are wasting away, yet inwardly we are being renewed day by day. For our light and momentary troubles are achieving for us an eternal glory that far outweighs them all. 2 Corinthians 4:16-17 (NIV)

WINGS LIKE EAGLES

Have you ever watched an eagle soaring in the sky? There is not a lot of frantic flapping of wings to stay aloft. It catches a current of air and soars, seemingly effortlessly. I watch in awe and wonder – is this what it's like to rest in God?

Not long ago I had the chance to experience that feeling. I was frantically going back and forth in my mind, trying to make a difficult decision. The choice I wanted to make didn't seem like it could provide what I thought I needed. The other one could provide on one level but was missing so much of what my heart wanted. What to do?

Finally I got smart and did what I should have in the first place. I prayed and left the answer in the hands of a loving God who truly knows what is best for me. The next morning when I opened my email there was a note from someone who didn't know anything about my struggle. This dear friend affirmed the decision that my heart had wanted to make. My prayer was answered in a totally unexpected way. I have no idea how all of the details will be worked out, but know that as I trust in God, everything will be fine.

"But those who trust in the Lord will find new strength. They will soar high on wings like eagles. They will run and not grow weary. They will walk and not faint." Isaiah 40:31 (NLT)

SPRING THAW

As I walked along the river bank, I came to a place that the spring thaw had not yet reached. It was an incredible experience to be able to hear the river flowing but to see nothing but ice. I wondered how many times my life has been like that. Have I not allowed others to see the vibrant life within me because it was buried beneath an uninviting layer of ice?

A short while later, as I climbed a hill, a loud sound was heard. Thinking a tree had fallen, I looked back at the river to see a large crack had formed a jagged opening down its center.

The water was breaking free of the icy grip that winter had placed upon it. Now that the warmth of the sun had exposed the water, it would, bit by bit, come to life again.

The same thing is true in my life. When I allow the love of Jesus, God's Son, to warm my heart, cracks start to appear in my cold exterior. With continued exposure I become a vibrant, flowing force that points people to the giver of life. When chunks of ice appear again, I only need to bring them to the light of the Son.

We ask this so that you will live the kind of lives that prove you belong to the Lord. Then you will want to please him in every way as you grow in producing every kind of good work by this knowledge about God. Colossians 1:10 (GWT)

Therefore, if anyone is in Christ, the new creation has come. The old has gone, the new is here! 2 Corinthians 5:17 (NIV)

BUMBLEBEES

Have you ever watched a bumblebee in flight? Laws of aerodynamics say that bumblebees don't have the capacity to achieve flight. In other words, they aren't shaped right for flight. Their bodies are too fat and heavy and their short wings should be incapable of lifting their heavy bodies. The fact is God gave them the power to fly, so they do. They haven't stopped to listen to those who say they can't.

How often do we not do something because somebody told us that it wasn't possible, or that we couldn't do it? Many before us have achieved great things that others told them were not possible. They just believed in themselves, learned from their mistakes and made it happen. I found a great quote from Henry Ford that sums this up: "Whether you think you can or think you can't – you're right." So, don't waste time listening to those who say you can't. Use the abilities that God has given you, take inspiration from the bumblebee, and get out there and do it.

Let us not become weary in doing good, for at the proper time we will reap a harvest if we do not give up. Galatians 6:9 (NIV)

For the Spirit God gave us does not make us timid, but gives us power, love and self-discipline. 2 Timothy 1:7 (NIV)

SHELTER

We planted a small rose bush this year. It had been several years since we had roses in our garden so this was a treat for us. Within weeks the plant beside it had flourished and the poor rose was being crowded out. It was then decided that we would move the rose to the very front of the yard as the accent in front of a large rock. Several days later when my husband said it needed water, I responded that it had just rained earlier that day. He told me that the rain was blowing and hadn't reached the rose since it was sheltered by the rock.

As I took in the meaning of his words, I repeated, "The rose was sheltered from the storm by the rock." It made me think of all the storms in my life that I have been sheltered from by my rock. God is the rock in my life that protects and saves me. When I rely on him, I am given strength to withstand the storms that inevitably come my way. There is no better shelter than that.

Truly he is my rock and my salvation; he is my fortress, I will not be shaken. Psalm 62:6 (NIV)

I keep my eyes always on the Lord. With him at my right hand, I will not be shaken. Psalm 16:8 (NIV)

HEAT WAVE

It was mid-July and we were in the first few days of a heat wave. The kind where it's too hot to be comfortable and it's also difficult to sleep as the temperature doesn't cool off at night. Summer was late arriving, but when it did come it was hard and fast. There was no gradual build up to the heat; no chance to slowly adjust to it. As I was sitting sweltering, I wondered how I could find value in this. It needed to be beyond the obvious of "things could be much worse" or "there are many who have suffered devastation with floods, tornados, fires, etc so we have nothing to complain about."

Maybe I could relate this to life. Many times there are things I want to do or accomplish, but it seems to take a long time to get to where I want to be. What if this is not a bad thing? Maybe getting there too quickly would bring about the same "shock to the system" that this sudden heat has. Perhaps I am not ready and need time to adjust. Instantly getting what I want, or what I think I want, isn't always good. If I am not properly prepared, things can become very uncomfortable. One step at a time will get me to where I want to be and I can take the time to enjoy the journey. What I need to remember is that just because I want something now does not mean that this is God's timing for me. Everything is in his perfect timing.

There is an opportune time to do things, a right time for everything on the earth. Ecclesiastes 3:1 (MSG)

GEESE

As seasons change and the weather cools down we see geese flying south for the winter. We hear their honking and see that familiar V formation in the sky.

I'm sure that most of us have heard the reasoning for this formation. Scientists have discovered that as each bird flaps its wings, it creates uplift for the bird immediately following. By flying in V formation, the whole flock adds at least 71% greater flying range than if each bird flew alone. If a goose falls out of formation, it feels the drag and resistance of flying alone and quickly rejoins the formation.

Did you know that the reason the geese honk from behind is to encourage the others to keep up their speed? Also, when the lead goose gets tired, it rotates back and another takes its place as lead.

There are so many lessons for us here. First, people sharing a common direction can get where they're going quicker and easier by traveling together. We should keep company with those heading in the same direction as us. Second, it makes sense to take turns doing the hard jobs and to remember to encourage those taking the lead.

Another thing about geese is when one gets sick or injured and falls out of formation, two others follow it down for protection and help. They stay together until it is either able to fly, or dead, and then they launch out again. They either fly on their own or join with another formation until they catch up to their group.

The final lesson here is to stand by each other. We should protect and care for each other. It is also good to make new friends who seem to be going in our direction.

If we allow God to lead us, as he leads the geese, how much better would our lives be?

He is our God and we are the people in his care, the flock that he leads.
Psalm 95:7 (GWT)

ECHOES

The definition of echo is "the reflection of a sound." Most of us have experimented with shouting "hello" and having the sound bounce back to us. This is a phenomena often heard in mountains and caverns.

When researching echoes, I found that to hear an echo clearly we need to be in an area that is closed and the wall that the sound bounces off should be more than 16.2 meters away. If the distance is less, we won't even notice the echo.

To a degree, this is also something we experience but seldom think about, in our everyday lives. In the confines of our minds, we tell ourselves many things. Often our thoughts are not even noticed by our conscious minds. The fact is that everything we say to ourselves comes back to us and reflects how we live our lives. Our negative thoughts are bouncing around in our heads and influencing our lives. Like echoes in the confines of a small space, we don't notice them, but they are there. If we tell ourselves we are not good enough, we will live our lives with a lack of confidence, afraid to tackle new challenges. If, on the other hand, we tell ourselves that we are valuable, we will go out into the world and accomplish far more than we ever imagined.

On my own I do not have the confidence, talents and abilities to achieve all of the things I would like to do. Instead of focusing on this, I need to remember that I am a child of God. He loves me and gives me the strength to do all things through him. He is the one who is able to accomplish much more through me than I had ever dreamed possible. When I see what He is doing in and through me, I know how much He values me. Looking at myself through His eyes is what I need to replace those negative echoes with positive ones.

I praise you because I am fearfully and wonderfully made; your works are wonderful, I know that full well. Psalm 139:14 (NIV)

MOUNTAIN LAKES

As we drove through the mountains we passed several lakes. One was a bit choppy from the breeze coming through the valley. The wind had stirred up some waves and the occasional white cap. Most of the lakes were calm with a few being so smooth that everything on the shoreline was reflected in them, like a giant mirror.

Gazing at these lakes, I realized that they had some good lessons for me. One of the things they teach is that it is best to stay calm. I am not nearly as inviting when I let things stir me up. When calm, I have the opportunity to make positive ripples.

Some of the lakes are crystal clear allowing me to see to the bottom. This reminds me to look below the surface. Things are not always what they seem at first glance.

The smooth, glass-like water has more than one message for me. The first one is that I need to take time to reflect. Sometimes in my busy life, I forget to do this. Even more important is to remember that it's God who calms my choppy waters. The more I come to him in prayer, the smoother my life becomes. He alone can calm the wind and the waves that stir up my discontent. The more I come to him, the more peaceful I become. This is what will enable me to reflect him to others.

He got up, rebuked the wind and said to the waves, "Quiet! Be still!" Then the wind died down and it was completely calm. Mark 4:39 (NIV)

Now we see things imperfectly, like puzzling reflections in a mirror, but then we will see everything with perfect clarity. All that I know now is partial and incomplete, but then I will know everything completely, just as God now knows me completely. 1 Corinthians 13:12 (NLT)

SEEDS

It came time to harvest the remaining vegetables from our garden. While we enjoy the taste of garden fresh vegetables, a big reason for planting the garden is for our grandchildren. They are excited to pull carrots, get them washed and then eat them with the tops still attached. Whenever they get the chance they like to pull their own, which many times results in the tops being in their hands while the carrot is still in the ground. This is particularly true of the larger carrots. Often there will be a large carrot and right next to it a small one.

How can this be? The seeds we planted were all the same, put side by side in the same soil, at the same time and cared for in exactly the same way. Yet they have not all matured at the same rate.

As I think about this I wonder, if this is true for seeds, isn't it also true for people? Deep within each of us we have many seeds. We have seeds of potential, of love and kindness; seeds of confidence and self-worth. We also have seeds of disappointment, of anger, of discouragement and low self-esteem. Some of these seeds grow larger and stronger than others, depending on which ones we focus.

No matter the seeds, they need the proper nourishment to grow and flourish. For me, I know that I have a choice to feed the negative seeds by focusing on them, or to let God nourish the positive seeds that He has planted in me.

As I look at the various sizes of carrots, side by side in my garden, I stop and wonder, which of the seeds in my life I am putting my focus on.

"What a person plants, he will harvest. The person who plants selfishness, ignoring the needs of others – ignoring God! – harvests a crop of weeds. All he'll have to show for his life is weeds! But the one who plants in response to God, letting God's Spirit do the growth work in him, harvests a crop of real life, eternal life" Galatians 6:7b-8 (MSG)

PIGEONS

We had pigeons attempting to make a home on an overhang of our roof. One Saturday morning the sound of their cooing woke us up much earlier than we had planned. My husband chased them off several times during the day, until they finally left for somewhere more hospitable.

At one point, as he was heading out to chase them again, I said, "If they'd only kept quiet we wouldn't have known they were there." In other words, they caused their own problems by not keeping quiet!

This is something that I'm sure I've done more often than I realize. It seems like my tongue is the hardest muscle in my body to control. When a thought pops into my head, I have a need to share it. Sometimes it's something that needs to be shared. Other times I speak before thinking and wish that I could take my words back. I heard an acronym that was WAIT – **W**hy **A**m **I** **T**alking? I need to remember this and to pray first and let God guide my thoughts and my words. When my words are prayerfully spoken, they can convey joy, love, compassion and encouragement. By doing this, my words will not cause problems but will have a positive impact.

People can tame all kinds of animals, birds, reptiles, and fish, but no one can tame the tongue. It is restless and evil, full of deadly poison. James 3:7,8 (NLT)

Before they call, I will answer. While they're still speaking, I will hear. Isaiah 65:24 (GWT)

OFF THE BEATEN PATH

As I walked toward the river I heard the gentle sound of the water, only audible when I listened carefully. The path veered off, but I wanted to be closer to the water, so stepped away from the regular path to get there.

Standing in the stillness, I listened to the sounds of nature around me. A sound I couldn't quite recognize was just to my right. I turned slightly and saw a squirrel in the branch of a tree just a little more than an arm's length away. It was happily munching on one of the small cones found on the forest floor. As it scurried back down the tree, I thought I had frightened it. Moments later, however, it was back on the branch with another cone.

What a gift it was to stand still and observe it so closely. Before I moved on, I thanked God for the gifts He shows me when I am willing to slow down and step off the beaten path.

He leads me beside quiet waters, he refreshes my soul. He guides me along the right paths for his name's sake. Psalm 23:2b,3 (NIV)

AUTUMN LEAVES

It is with mixed emotion that I look at the leaves changing colour. Once a lush green, they are changing to gold, orange and red. Their beauty against a backdrop of clear blue sky can be breathtaking. As the breeze blows, the rustle of the dry leaves can be heard as they are released from their branches and flutter to the ground. They crunch under our feet as we walk. They can also be gathered into piles that children and the young at heart love to jump into.

This is a beautiful time of year. The sun still shines brightly but without the intense heat. The morning and evening air has a crispness about it that feels so refreshing. As the days get noticeably shorter we have to face the fact that the long, lazy days of summer have come to an end.

So it is with the seasons of our lives. None of them last forever. This is a relief sometimes and a disappointment others. We need to find the beauty of the season we are in and enjoy today. If I spend today dreading the coming winter, I will miss the beauty of today and all of the colours it has to offer me.

There is a time for everything, and a season for every activity under the heavens. Ecclesiastes 3:1(NIV)

SILENCE

I was attending a silent retreat. While I was not speaking, things were far from silent. Sitting in the morning sunshine I was serenaded by the songs of various birds. Some I would have noticed before, but there are many I would have missed amid the sounds of human voices.

Even though I was not speaking aloud, the voices in my head continued. Random thoughts appeared in my conscious mind, taking me back to the busy life I'd left behind. It was during these times that I realized how difficult it is to focus on only the present.

I gazed over an expanse of lawn, framed by towering evergreens. Off to one side, a river wound its way lazily through the property. I was surrounded by the beauty and majesty that God had created. In my mind I heard the words "be still and know that I am God." It is in the stillness that God's message for me becomes clear. For only when I block out the distractions of the world am I truly able to focus on the loving relationship that my Heavenly Father longs to have with me. There is peace, stillness for my mind and renewal for my soul to be found in the silence.

He says, "Be still, and know that I am God; I will be exalted among the nations, I will be exalted in the earth." Psalm 46:10 (NIV)

WINGS TO FLY

One day we spent some time watching a family of birds in our yard. It all started with hearing a bird crying for help. That was not the normal, happy song we associate with our feathered friends, so we went to investigate. As we watched, we saw a baby bird come out from a bush in our front yard. It managed to get up onto a planter but then cried for the parents to come to the rescue. As they would approach, it would flutter its tiny wings, but wouldn't move from its perch. When the parents would land, they would be met with an open mouth, demanding to be fed. Throughout the day this scene was repeated many times, in several areas of the yard. We could see the parents attempting to teach the little one how to fly. Despite their example and encouragement, it appeared too frightened to take the risk.

We said to each other, "There's a lesson for us here." Often we find ourselves in the same position as this baby bird. We get comfortable in our little routine. When it comes time to try something new we get stuck in our fear and can't move ahead. Thoughts like: "Why can't you just keep on doing it for me?" "I don't want to do it myself;" "Spreading my wings to fly is far too scary;" and "What if I can't do it?" go through our minds. Like the baby bird, we want to stick with what we know. It is much easier to rely on someone else to take care of us than to take the responsibility for our own nourishment. The only problem with this is that it keeps us on the ground when, with a little effort, we could be soaring.

We saw this family of birds a week or so later. It was exciting to see the three of them fly into our back yard and land on the fence. The baby took the risk, learned from the example of others and is now flying. Here we see our lesson for life. We are all capable of soaring, but first have to be willing to risk taking that leap of faith. It may not happen for us the first time we try, but as we learn from our mistakes we grow stronger and more confident. Soon we will be spreading our wings to fly.

Have I not commanded you? Be strong and courageous. Do not be afraid; do not be discouraged, for the Lord your God will be with you wherever you go." Joshua 1:9 (NIV)

Inspirations From Around the House

RECIPES

I decided to try a new recipe. We both felt like lasagna would be a good meal, but as I have some food issues, this wasn't going to be as easy as it sounded. I searched online for a gluten and dairy free recipe and found one that looked promising.

We picked up the necessary ingredients and made a meal that was a real treat for me. I posted online that I had tried this new recipe and really enjoyed it. Little did I realize that this would be one of my more popular posts! Requests for the recipe started coming in. As I was sending it off, I commented to someone that, while being gluten and dairy free is a challenge, if I want something badly enough I can usually find a way to make it happen.

Those words struck me and I thought of a quote my husband had used in a presentation the night before: "If you really want to do something, you'll find a way. If you don't, you'll find an excuse." (Jim Rohn). How true that is in my life. I tend to be very good at making excuses. Is it the same for you? Do you think about things you want to do but find yourself making excuses? This awareness has caused me to think about how to make a way, instead of an excuse. When I pray and ask the Lord for guidance, I don't need excuses. He is the one who can show me the way. My recipe for lasagna also reminded me of an important recipe for life!

Taste and see that the Lord is good. Blessed is the person who takes refuge in him. Psalm 34:8 (NIV)

INGREDIENTS

Looking in my pantry I see a wide variety of items. Ingredients for many types of recipes are contained there. When I decide to make cookies, I will use the flour, sugar, shortening, and probably the chocolate chips. The vinegar, curry powder and Tabasco sauce have their place in other dishes, but would not be good additions to my cookies. The ingredients I choose are important to the success of what I am making.

The same is true with my life. When I wake up in the morning I can choose the ingredients that will shape my day. If I throw together bitterness, self pity and anger, my day will reflect this and will not be pleasant. If I blend together faith, gratitude, love and acceptance, my day will be much more positive. During the day, as circumstances change, the ingredients may need to be adjusted so that the desired outcome may still be achieved. I have found that a sprinkling of humor at points during the day is also helpful.

One thing that I have realized is that when I start my day with prayer, the other ingredients for my successful day are much easier to come by. I don't have to go out and look for them, I just pray for the strength and grace to handle whatever comes my way. The ingredients that I consciously choose to add to my day will directly affect the outcome, so I need to choose wisely.

Do not be anxious about anything, but in every situation, by prayer and petition, with thanksgiving, present your request to God. And the peace of God, which transcends all understanding, will guard your hearts and minds in Christ Jesus. Philippians 4:6,7 (NIV)

BROKEN DISHES

It started out like any other time I emptied the dishwasher. Our plates were heavy and it was always an effort to lift a stack of them onto the second shelf in the cupboard. The difference this time was that they didn't quite make it! Just before they reached the shelf, they inexplicably came crashing down around me. As I stood in disbelief watching them fall and shatter, I somehow had the presence of mind to take a step backwards and not get struck by the jagged shards landing around me.

Six out of eight plates were broken, one was chipped around the edges and one remained intact. I'm still not sure how it all happened but it definitely made a mess. After checking to make sure I was alright, my husband helped me clean up the pieces and joked that if we had company over, we'd have to eat in shifts and wash the plates in between. We both understood that it was no use getting upset because that wouldn't do a thing to change the situation.

I have been striving to create value in all things, so have been thinking about the lesson for me in this. Other than having a good story to tell, what did I learn? Perhaps in my haste I often take on a little more than I can carry. If I lighten the load it will take me longer. Frequently I struggle with something, certain I can handle it, when it would not only be much simpler but also more efficient to either ask for help or divide the load.

This was a dramatic way to illustrate the point, but I think I finally understand it. Instead of thinking I can handle everything on my own, I need to stop and pray about it. Once I share my burden with Christ, it becomes much lighter.

"So do not fear, for I am with you; do not be dismayed, for I am your God. I will strengthen you and help you; I will uphold you with my righteous right hand." Isaiah 41:10 (NIV)

LIKE SILVER

As I polished silver, I found great satisfaction in restoring the shine. All I had to do was rub it with a polishing cloth and soon the discolouration was gone and I could see my reflection.

It reminded me of a story I'd read several years ago. A woman called a silversmith and made an appointment to watch him at work. As she watched, the silversmith held a piece of silver over the fire letting it heat up. He explained that when refining silver, one needed to hold the silver in the middle of the fire where the flames were hottest to burn away all the impurities. She asked him if he had to sit in front of the fire the whole time the silver was being refined. The man answered that not only did he have to sit there holding the silver, but he had to keep his eyes on it the entire time it was in the fire. If the silver was left even a moment too long in the flames, it would be destroyed. After thinking for a few moments, she asked "How do you know when the silver is fully refined?" He smiled at her and answered, "Oh, that's easy – when I see my image in it."

This is what life is like. Sometimes we are put in the fire so the impurities can rise to the surface and be removed. Sometimes it seems we are being rubbed far too hard. God uses these experiences to refine and polish us. If you are going through the heat of the fire right now, remember that God is not only holding you, but His eye is on you constantly. Our refining process will only be complete when His image can be seen in us.

He will sit as a refiner and purifier of silver; Malachi 3:3a (NIV)

PHOTOGRAPHS

I had spent some time looking at family photographs. Some are very old, quite small and in black and white. Others are more recent, much larger in size and in full colour. One thing they all have in common is that they were taken before the digital camera gave us instant images.

In the days of these pictures, film was loaded into a camera. Once the roll of film was full, it was developed in a dark room from negatives. Looking at these negatives, an outline of the picture can be seen, but it isn't the clear picture that we'll see after the developing has been completed.

Life can be like this. There have been many days that I stared at the negatives in my life, wondering how they could possibly develop into a picture I could be happy with. Sometimes it felt like I was in that dark room. Over time, my picture became more focused and no longer a shadowy outline. This is something that I need to remember. When life is full of negatives and I'm in a dark place, I need to trust that God is using this to develop my life into a beautiful picture that he can be proud of.

We also glory in our sufferings, because we know that suffering produces perseverance; perseverance, character; and character, hope. And hope does not put us to shame, because God's love has been poured out into our hearts through the Holy Spirit, who has been given to us. Romans 5:3-5 (NIV)

PRISMATIC

I have a sun catcher on the window by my front door. When the sun hits it at the right angle, it sends multicoloured spots on the surrounding surfaces. My grandchildren are fascinated by these and love to try to touch them. In another area we have some stained glass picture frames that also project these coloured spots on the ceiling when the sun hits them just right.

The effect of these is quite lovely. It is prismatic. One of the definitions of prismatic is brilliantly coloured, iridescent or exhibiting spectral colours formed by refraction of light through a prism. In essence this means that when the sun shines on it the light is refracted in colours onto another surface.

This morning I was struck by a thought as I admired the colours on my wall, then looked for the surface the sun was shining on to create this effect. When the light of the Son, Jesus, shines on me, what image is projected for others to see? Do I simply absorb the light or do I send it back into the world in bright colours that inspire others to look for the source of this light?

"In the same way, let your good deeds shine out for all to see, so that everyone will praise your heavenly Father." Matthew 5:16 (NLT)

RECYCLING

Recycling is the environmentally friendly thing to do. We have bins in our garage for newspapers, plastic and metal. We also make sure to take our bottles, cans and milk cartons to the bottle depot. It takes a conscious effort, but is worth it in the long run. The items we recycle can be reprocessed and made into something useful, rather than piling up as garbage. It has become so much a part of our lives that I don't realize the impact it has until I visit an area that doesn't have recycling facilities and see the garbage that is littering the sides of roads. So many things that have the potential to be useful are just left to turn into an eyesore.

Have you ever stopped to consider that many things that cause us pain in life can also be recycled? When we can look back on them objectively and see the lessons learned, we are, in effect, taking our garbage and recycling it into something of value. So, when you're filling your recycling bins, mentally fill one with the wounds and trials you have experienced. Then, give it to God and watch to see what He can turn this into for you.

So we're not giving up. How could we! Even though on the outside it often looks like things are falling apart on us, on the inside, where God is making new life, not a day goes by without his unfolding grace. These hard times are small potatoes compared to the coming good times, the lavish celebration prepared for us. There's far more here than meets the eye. The things we see now are here today, gone tomorrow. But the things we can't see now will last forever. 2 Corinthians 4:16-18 (MSG)

WEIGHT LOSS

I've often heard it said that you should only weigh yourself in the morning and never at night. This is something I wondered about so decided to try an experiment. Before going to bed I weighed myself and then did so again when I got up in the morning. Much to my surprise there was a two pound difference! This got me wondering, where does that weight go while we sleep? I may never know the answer to that but it reminded me of another type of weight loss.

Also weighing me down are the burdens I carry from my daily life. They can be heavy and uncomfortable, making me weary through the day. At night, they weigh heavily on my mind, making sleep difficult. When I take these and pray about them before going to bed, they're taken from my mind and not only do I sleep better, but I wake up with a much lighter, brighter attitude. This makes me more pleasant to be around and also gives me renewed energy to get through the day. It seems to me that this is the best weight loss program I can follow.

Now to him who is able to do immeasurably more than all we ask or imagine, according to his power that is at work within us, to him be glory in the church and in Christ Jesus throughout all generations, for ever and ever! Amen. Ephesians 3:20,21 (NIV)

Inspirations While Out and About

SHOULDER RIDES

We enjoyed a trip to Orlando with family. Visiting theme parks is fun, but also tiring, especially for young children. It's also difficult for them to see what's going on when most around them are so much taller. When the younger children were tired or wanted a better view, dad or granddad would lift them onto their shoulders. Sometimes the children asked for this. Other times their needs were sensed and they were scooped up. Either way, sitting up there was a wonderful place to be. There were times when, feeling hot and tired, I wished that I could have a shoulder ride as well!

It was then I realized that this is something God does for me on a regular basis. When I am too tired to keep going, he carries me until I regain my strength. There are times that I can't see to move forward. This is when he lifts me up so I can know what direction I should be heading in. Sometimes I am lifted to see something wonderful he wants to show me. God knows what I need and when I need it. There are times he waits for me to ask but many times the lift I get is an unexpected gift. I take great comfort in knowing that my Heavenly Father is always there looking out for me.

Yet to all who did receive him, to those who believed in his name, he gave the right to become children of God. John 1:12 (NIV)

The Lord is good to all; he has compassion on all he has made. Psalm 145:9 (NIV)

DON'T ROCK THE BOAT

We watched people floating down the river on tubes, air mattresses and in small inflatable boats. It looked like fun so we decided to try it. The first run was a short 10 minutes to make sure the kids were OK. Since there wasn't enough room for everyone in the boats, I volunteered to walk along the path and take pictures. You see, I loved the idea of being in a boat, but have a fear of the water. The river was not deep and was slow moving, but what if I tipped? What if it was more difficult than it looked?

My longing for the adventure overtook my fear and I asked to go along when a few decided on the longer, 1 hour trip. My first challenge was getting into the small inflatable boat. It just wasn't going to hold still for me! "Don't rock the boat" is something I have lived with for a long time. It hasn't served me well in life and it certainly wasn't helping here. The boat rocked and tipped a little, letting in water as I got in. It was only uncomfortable for a minute and I soon forgot all about the puddle of water I was sitting in. After floating a bit, I got caught on rocks in a shallow area. In order to free myself, I had to 'rock the boat' again. Soon I relaxed and enjoyed the ride with the clear blue sky above, the tall evergreens flanking the river and the peaceful surroundings.

The ride was not all smooth. There were a few areas of swifter water, more rocks to get hung up on and hazards in the water to avoid. My companions seemed to navigate this more smoothly than I did, but that was alright. It was all part of the journey and I loved every minute of it. Sometimes I could float easily on the current, sometimes I had to fight to keep going the right way and sometimes I had to rock the boat. Sounds a lot like life, doesn't it? My one hour trip down the river reminded me that life does not always flow the way I expect it to. There will be hazards to avoid and places where I get temporarily stuck. Most of all, I learned that these are all part of the adventure and sometimes rocking the boat is what is needed to keep moving forward.

Let go of your concerns! Then you will know that I am God. I rule the nations. I rule the earth. Psalm 46:10 (GWT)

FITTING IN

While wandering through a store one day, I saw a sign that said, "Why are you trying so hard to fit in when you were born to stand out?"

This really got me to thinking. I have spent my life trying to fit in, wanting to be like everyone else. When I stop to think of the people I admire, they are not the same as everyone else. They have a unique quality about them. I can admire them and learn from them, but I can't be just like them. I need to be me. Here come the insecurities – "What if me, isn't enough?"

I saw another poster that said: "I don't want to 'fit in'. I want to stand out. I want the world to know I was here, that I made a difference." That resonates with me. God made each of us unique. Every finger on every hand of every person on earth has its own unique fingerprint. We have each been given our own talents and abilities to use for His purposes. We also have our own strengths and weaknesses. Realizing that no two of us are exactly alike, I need to embrace this instead of trying hard to be like everyone else. Each of us has a very distinct role to play and if my focus is being like someone else, there will be no one to fill my role. After all, if we were all exactly alike, some of us wouldn't be needed!

Have I not commanded you? Be strong and courageous. Do not be afraid; do not be discouraged, for the Lord your God will be with you wherever you go. Joshua 1:9 (NIV)

CARRY THE LOAD

My husband and I stopped to pick up a few things for dinner. He was carrying the basket and stopped to put it down while checking something out. As I reached to take it from him, he said it was OK, he'd just put it down. Saying that I didn't mind, I reached for it again. When he asked me why I should carry this heavy basket when he could set it down to rest, my mind shifted gears.

It suddenly struck me how many times I feel it necessary to take someone's burden and carry it for them when all they want to do is to set it down. I may think that I'm being helpful, but sometimes I'm actually hindering the process of letting go. The same holds true when I want to set down the heavy load I'm carrying and someone else offers to hold it for me until I have the strength to carry it again. We all need to set our burdens and heavy loads down at the feet of Jesus and leave them there.

Who would have thought that a simple trip to the grocery store would have reminded me of such an important life lesson?

"Come to me, all who are tired from carrying heavy loads and I will give you rest." Matthew 11:28 (GWT)

CRAYONS

I saw a wall hanging that had a few crayons pictured and the words, "Be the brightest colour in the box." The letters were in many bright colours and it captured not only my attention but also my imagination.

Crayons have a lot to teach us. They come in assorted colours. Some are bright and stand out, while others tend to blend in with the background. In the larger boxes, there are ones with exotic sounding names. Some are fresh and sharp. There are others that are worn, broken and have their wrappers in tatters. Being well loved has had this effect on some, while it is the lack of care and respect that has done this to others.

The lesson for me is that although these crayons are very different, they can all co-exist in the same container. Not only that, but they make people happy just by being themselves. I'm pretty certain that the red crayon doesn't think it needs to be like the yellow one to be appreciated.

The same is true for people. I am not the same as everyone around me and don't need to colour my world in the same way as others do. There is also no need to fear or envy those who are different. God created us in many sizes, shapes and colours. Each of us has been gifted in ways that make us unique. I am the only one that can use my particular gifts to bring the colour and light that God has planned for those He brings into my life.

Each of you should use whatever gift you have received to serve others, as faithful stewards of God's grace in its various forms. 1 Peter 4:10 (NIV)

NAMETAGS

It was an interesting week for me. As I was getting ready to head out of town for some speaking engagements, I could feel the beginnings of a cold coming on. Not willing to succumb to it, I took large doses of Echinacea, hoping the cold would not materialize.

When I arrived at my first destination, I was given a nametag to wear. I felt strong and confident as I put on the tag with my name. It could have read "confident in my abilities" as that's how I felt. The next morning I knew I was losing my voice but was determined not to let that stop me as I headed off to speak at a brunch. Putting on my nametag there, I was less confident in my abilities and relying on God to keep my voice strong. Instead of my name, this tag could have read "relying on God." By the time I was ready to speak again that evening my voice was almost non-existent. If I was relying on my own strength, my nametag would have said "defeated." Instead, I surrendered totally to God, knowing that, on my own, I didn't possess the strength to share His message tonight. My nametag at that time should have read "totally surrendered." I prayed that my voice would be restored. However, that wasn't the plan that God had in mind. Instead, my hoarse and cracked voice kept going, and though it sounded like it would give out, it never totally did. What I received was enough strength to persevere, but not enough that it would appear to anyone I was doing this on my own.

This was a physical reminder that the nametag I wear for the world to see, directly affects what I can accomplish. When I am not feeling strong or confident in my abilities I have the choice to wear my "defeated" or "can't do that" nametag or to consciously choose to wear the nametag "totally surrendered to God." Not only can I rest in his strength, but that is also when he does his best work through me.

I can do everything through Christ who strengthens me. Philippians 4:13 (GWT)

HAPPIEST PLACE

Our family went on vacation to what is often referred to as 'the happiest place on earth'. While this is the way people think of this special destination as they are planning their vacations, the reality that I saw there was a little different.

It was hot and young children were often tired and complaining. Frustrated parents were demanding that the kids have a good time. This was not a good combination.

Height restrictions for certain rides were what caused the problems for us. Our youngest grandchild was measured at the entrance to a ride and met the height standards. After waiting in line, we were just boarding the ride when someone decided to pull her out and measure her again. She was upset and afraid and shrunk down a little, which resulted in her not being allowed on the ride with the rest of the family. Her granddad stayed with her and did his best to comfort a sobbing little girl who kept saying, "I'm not big enough." This was the note that our visit to 'the happiest place on earth' ended on.

All of this just reinforced for us that the happiest place is not a location, but when we are walking with Jesus. He will never turn us away because we don't measure up to the standards set by others. He has paid the price, so that in God's eyes we always measure up.

So we can go confidently to the throne of God's kindness to receive mercy and find kindness, which will help us at the right time. Hebrews 4:16 (GWT)

POOL NOODLES

I participate in an aqua fit class at our local pool. Often, for extra resistance in the water we use either barbells or noodles that are made of dense foam. The facility had just purchased some new pool noodles and our class was the first to use them. They had a slightly waxy, slightly greasy feel to them. This will lessen with use but this day it made them much more difficult to hold onto. During one exercise the instructor said "this is so greasy, I almost lost my grip."

My mind shifted gears immediately as I thought of several sayings I have heard over the years. If I hear "get a grip on yourself" it means that I have to make a better effort to control my emotions or behavior. When I need to "get a grip on something" it means I need a better understanding of what is going on. When I "lose my grip", it means I have lost control.

My struggle is with control. I have a tendency to want to control what goes on in my life. The problem is that excessive control doesn't lead to a peaceful life. When I give control of my life to Jesus, life is so much better. I have learned that this isn't something that I can do once and then relax. Giving up control needs to be done daily, hourly and sometimes minute by minute. When I give full control to Jesus, the contentment floods my soul and I am at peace.

Let go [of your concerns]! Then you will know that I am God. I rule the nations. I rule the earth. Psalm 46:10 (GWT)

NOT WHAT I EXPECTED

Have you ever made a decision that seemed right at the time only to be met with an expected challenge that left you wondering about your choice? That doesn't necessarily mean the decision was wrong. Maybe the challenge was needed and this was the only way to face it.

That describes an experience I had. We were on vacation and needed to make a choice between two churches to go to the next morning. After doing a little research online, I made the decision by picking the one that seemed the most like what I was used to. Upon arrival we soon discovered that my choice was definitely not what I was familiar with! Being there challenged me on many levels and I was way out of my comfort zone. My first instinct was to leave and find somewhere more comfortable. Knowing that wasn't possible, I needed to make the best of it. After relaxing a bit, I actually started to enjoy myself. Seeing how much others were getting out of this service reminded me anew that there are many ways to do things. My way is not right for everyone. Appreciating the methods of others can be very enlightening.

I had spent the previous days trying to figure out what to write about in my weekly blog. There were many thoughts going through my head, but I was trying too hard and nothing was coming together. I strongly believe that God gives me the words and experiences to share. When I got out of my comfortable situation and stopped trying so hard, God gave me several ideas to write about. Maybe He just needed to shake me up a little to get my attention! My experience was not at all what I expected, but I ended getting so much out of it, that it was exactly what I needed.

But to all who believed him and accepted him, he gave the right to become children of God. John 1:12 (NLT)

PANIC BUTTON

One morning I parked my car in a spot that left me very little space to squeeze out of the door. As I did so, I inadvertently pressed the panic button on my key fob. The horn started honking, the lights flashing and I was caught unaware and didn't know what to do. My first instinct was to hit the panic button again to turn it off. That didn't work. I squeezed back into the car and started it, thinking this would cancel the alarm. No success. I locked and unlocked the car, still with no success. Thinking that maybe starting it and driving would help, I drove to another parking spot. The alarm kept going. As I sat in my noisy vehicle, trying to think what to do next, the alarm suddenly stopped. It must have been set to go for a certain amount of time and then shut off. With relief, I headed off to my exercise class.

As I left the class an hour later I started to think about that panic button and how often I push the panic button in my life when it isn't necessary. Pushing it again doesn't negate the chain of events that I have started. It's not something that can be erased so as to start again. Just as with my car, the error in pushing the panic button in life causes confusion and disruption. Frantically trying to restore things to normal doesn't always improve the situation. Sometimes there's nothing that can be done but wait it out until calm returns. Maybe this little accident with the panic button was not so much an accident but a life lesson for me. Instead of reacting in panic, I can turn to God and let him take care of things for me.

But in my distress I cried out to the Lord; yes, I prayed to my God for help. He heard me from his sanctuary; my cry reached his ears. Psalm 18:6 (NLT)

DUCK RACES

We spent a fun filled weekend camping with our family. Three days with no cell phones or internet, just face to face contact with the people who mean the most to us. It was wonderful.

One of the things we did at the campground was to go to the river and watch the duck races. About 50 rubber duckies were numbered and then dropped together into the river. A little farther down the river people were waiting to catch them and see which ones finished in the top three spots. It was surprising to see how spread out these ducks became.

What a good picture of life this was. Even though we may start out in the river of life at the same place, some of us get caught up in currents that rush us along. Others get caught in rocky places and need help to get going again. A few choose to meander along close to shore. Eventually we reach our destination, each following the current of life that directs their way.

This was a reminder to me that though I may think that I set my own course, it's God's plan for my life that ultimately guides me.

O Lord, my God, you have performed many wonders for us. Your plans for us are too numerous to list. Psalm 40:5 (NLT)

GARAGE SALES

"Look, there are a lot of garage sales over there" I said. After a quick look in that direction, my husband said, "I don't see any." To which I replied, "Things you're looking for aren't always in plain sight, sometimes you have to follow the signs to get to them." As soon as the words were spoken, we knew that this applied to our lives. Sometimes there are signs pointing in more than one direction and we have to make the decision on which one to follow. Some of the signs are small and others are eye catching in fluorescent colours or with balloons attached.

The signs lead us on a treasure hunt. They take us to things that others are discarding which just may be of value to us. We are willing to search for these signs and follow where they lead on the chance that they take us to treasure and not trash. It is a risk we are willing to take.

There are other signs in our lives that always lead us to treasure. They are not flashy but are the right ones to follow to find the rich, fulfilling life we seek. The signs of love, forgiveness and grace that Jesus has left for us let us know that we are treasured and will never be discarded. These are the ones we need to seek. Once we find them, we are better able to reflect them to others and point them to the greatest treasure the world has ever known.

May the Lord direct your lives as you show God's love and Christ's endurance. 2 Thessalonians 3:5 (GWT)

My sheep listen to my voice: I know them and they follow me. I give them eternal life, and they shall never perish; no one can snatch them out of the Father's hand. John 10:27,28 (NIV)

Inspirations From the Seashore

ABUNDANCE

I have discovered that a great place to search for shells is in the shallow waters of a fishing area. There are an abundance of them. Some are scattered and easy to spot as they sit on their own. Most, however, are in large deposits, sometimes in a few close groupings and other times in trails that stretch across the sand. The more I pay attention and look for them, the more I find.

They remind me of the blessings in my life. I am aware of a few scattered here and there, but when I stop and really look, I can see them everywhere. There are clusters of them and trails that stretch throughout my life. The sheer abundance of them is staggering. So much so, that it's easy to take them for granted.

Every day I want to take the time to stop and appreciate my blessings and to thank God for the gifts that he has given to me.

Praise the God and Father of our Lord Jesus Christ! Through Christ, God has blessed us with every spiritual blessing that heaven has to offer. Ephesians 1:3 (GWT)

AS FAR AS THE EYE CAN SEE

As I gaze out over the deck, there is an unbroken line of sea, stretching out to meet the sky. I wonder how far it is that I can see. If I look to the west, I can see a long pier that is about 15 km from us. Today there is a cruise ship docked there. It looks very small from this distance, but I can see it and know that it's there.

In the evening we take a walk and once away from the lights, look up at the sky. The dark sky is illuminated by a dazzling array of stars. The longer we stand looking, the more we can see. These are farther away than I can fathom, and yet they can be seen all these millions of miles away on earth.

God created all of this for us – the earth, the seas and the heavens. The earth and the seas have boundaries and measurements. The heavens, however, are infinite, just as God is in his wisdom and love. That's why, when I'm looking for answers or guidance, the natural place for me to look is heavenward, to Him. No distance is too far for Him to reach out to me.

"For my thoughts are not your thoughts, neither are your ways my ways," declares the Lord. "As the heavens are higher than the earth, so are my ways higher than your ways and my thoughts than your thoughts." Isaiah 55:8,9 (NIV)

BROKEN

As I walked along the shore I picked up some shells that had been broken, exposing the inner parts that would not normally be seen. It was interesting to see that there was very little debris, such as clumps of sand or tiny fragments of broken shell, inside. They had been washed clean and dried by the warmth of the sun. Other shells, the ones that appeared intact, had this debris, or garbage, visible at their opening and must have had more trapped in the areas that were not visible.

This got me to thinking. Did I have a tough shell around me? One that is not only hiding the garbage inside so no one sees it, but also preventing this debris from being washed away? When was the last time I cracked open that shell and let anyone see what was really inside of me? Maybe it's time to open up and let the waves of God's love wash away the silt inside of me and the light of His Son warm me. Then, there will be no need to fear if others can see through the cracks into a heart that is exposed. Its imperfections will have been cleansed and its inner beauty revealed.

For you were once darkness. But now you are light in The Lord.
Ephesians 5:8 (NIV)

DIVERSITY

After two weeks of beach walks, I ended up with a large collection of shells. Some are delicate like bone china, others are thick and calloused. There are all sizes, ranging from very tiny to large and heavy. The colours range from white to pink, orange, brown and green with some having several colours in them. There are some that are made more interesting by their scars and some that look perfect on the outside.

Just as there is diversity in these shells, so it is with people. We come in all shapes, sizes and colours. Some only show the world their perfect side and others draw us to them by the story behind their scars. There is a collective beauty that we all add our part to.

The amazing thing is that we are each loved by God as the unique creations he designed us to be. It reminds me of a song I learned in childhood "red and yellow, black and white, all are precious in his sight. Jesus loves the little children of the world." This is such a good reminder for me. He loves each of us as if there was only one of us. The diversity or difference is all part of his plan, so I need to remember and embrace this.

There are different spiritual gifts, but the same Spirit gives them. There are different ways of serving, and yet the same Lord is served. There are different types of work to do, but the same God produces every gift in every person. 1 Corinthians 12:4-6 (GWT)

EBB AND FLOW

We stood in the shallow water with only our ankles and feet getting wet. With every wave we would watch the shells tumble towards shore, and then get pulled back out again in the crystal clear water. Sometimes we spotted a shell we wanted a closer look at, but if we weren't quick enough it would disappear before we could reach for it. The next wave may bring it back or it may now be buried under a layer of sand.

So it is with us. I have been tossed to and fro as the troubles of life hit and shake things up. Sometimes I get buried for awhile or washed out to sea temporarily. Sooner or later the ebb and flow will wash away the sand, clean off the debris and deposit me back on the dry beach where I can feel the warmth of the sun shining on me again. I just have to remember that I am always in the loving care of God and that he will guide me through the turmoil. When I look back on the troubled times, it is his guidance and the lessons learned during this time that will be remembered.

The Lord is good, a refuge in times of trouble. He cares for those who trust in him, Nahum 1:7 (NIV)

EROSION

The beach we enjoy walking along is slowly being reclaimed by the tides. Some areas that we used to walk have now become impassable. In others we have to carefully choose a path to get through. The timing for our walks needs to coincide with the tide schedule.

Some formerly gentle slopes have been sheared off, exposing the roots of the vegetation still clinging there. As we rounded a bend one day, we saw 2 houses with their retaining walls crumbling. No doubt this damage did not happen overnight but bit by bit as the sea slowly encroached on the formerly dry land.

This kind of erosion can take place in our lives as well. Bit by bit, negativity erodes our self confidence and slowly chips away at our quality of life. It happens so slowly that we don't realize it. One day we wake up and wonder how we got so far off track. Next we question how to find our way back.

For me, I need to reconnect with God's instruction book. When I read my Bible, I am reminded anew that He has a wonderful plan for my life. Then I pray and let Him guide me back to where I need to be.

"For I know the plans I have for you," declares the Lord, "plans to prosper you and not to harm you, plans to give you hope and a future." Jeremiah 29:11 (NIV)

FEAST OR FAMINE

We heard a loud squawking overhead and looked up to see two gulls. The loud one was following closely behind one with a fish in its beak, obviously wanting a share of this catch. As we watched, a much larger bird circled and then swooped down, attempting to steal the fish. From what we could see, the fish was dropped back into the water and none of the birds got to enjoy it for a meal.

Several times we had seen fishing boats that had flocks of birds hovering around them, hoping to get some of the catch for themselves.

There are times in life when I have been in each of these positions. Sometimes I have worked hard and have known others were waiting to take away what was mine. Many times I have gladly shared my abundance with those around me. Then there are the times I'm not so proud of. Times when I hovered nearby hoping to get something from those that were successful.

As long as I depend, not on handouts, but on the fruits of my labors, I know that God will supply my every need.

Then he said to them, "Watch out! Be on your guard against all kinds of greed; life does not consist in an abundance of possessions." Luke 12:15 (NIV)

FISHERMEN

While in Mexico we stopped to watch some fishermen not far from shore. Their boat was like an overgrown rowboat with an outboard motor on the back. The motor had been lifted out of the water and they used a long pole to maneuver the boat in the shallow water. The net they were hauling in was so large that it took two or three of them to pull it closer. We saw one of the men give a flick of the wrist and a streak of silver flew out of the net and into the boat. Another man gathered the fish up. The net got caught a few times and if poking at it with the long pole didn't work, someone would jump out of the boat to free it.

This was not sport fishing we were observing. These men, and many others like them, earn their livelihood by fishing these waters. It was nothing like the modern commercial fishing we would see in Canada. The picture it paints for me is one of Biblical times, when Jesus met fishermen and said, "Follow me; I will make you fishers of men."

I am forever grateful that I was scooped up in his net and put in the boat with him. My life has not been the same since and now my desire is to bring others alongside and into his boat. There is no better place to be.

As Jesus was walking beside the Sea of Galilee, he saw two brothers; Simon called Peter and his brother Andrew. They were casting a net into the lake, for they were fishermen. "Come, follow me," Jesus said, "and I will make you fishers of men." At once they left their nets and followed him. Matthew 4:18-20 (NIV)

FLAMINGOS

There is an area in the Mexican state of Yucatan that is known as the main courtship area for greater pink flamingos during the fall and winter. You need to contract a boat to go to the ria to see them. There are warnings not to get too close. We are told that the flamingos can break their necks or wings if they are frightened into flight.

The thought strikes me "How often have I taken off at breakneck speeds when I perceived danger?" Is my sense of danger on high alert, causing me to react first and deal with the consequences later? Perhaps I need to learn to relax and be more trusting. Very little of what comes my way will make it necessary for me to react with such panic. I'm fairly certain that none of it is worth breaking my neck over. I need to stop, pray about the situation and let God direct me.

The Lord is my light and my salvation. Who is there to fear? The Lord is my life's fortress. Who is there to be afraid if? Psalm 27:1 (GWT)

FOOTPRINTS IN THE SAND

As we walked along the shore I asked, "Will you take a picture of my footprints in the sand?" I was on the hard packed sand next to the water's edge when I stepped out in front to make the footprints. As my husband got the camera ready, a wave came in and my footprints were washed away.

We talked about how fast our footprints disappear on the hard packed, easy to walk on sand. If we walked a little farther up from the shoreline, the sand was much softer. It wasn't as easy to walk here, but the footprints went much deeper into the sand and we could still see the ones we had made when we passed this way earlier.

So it is with life. When we walk the easy route our footprints are shallow and easily get washed away. When we take the more challenging route, our impression goes deeper and is longer lasting. My goal is to leave a lasting impression so that one day my grandchildren will have evidence that I was here. Perhaps my footprints can even help to guide them at times they aren't sure of their way. That is the kind of legacy I want to leave.

That's why we live with such good cheer. You won't see us drooping our heads or dragging our feet! 2 Corinthians 5:7 (MSG)

Don't become like the people of this world. Instead, change the way you think. Then you will always be able to determine what God really wants – what is good, pleasing, and perfect. Romans 12:2 (GWT)

GARBAGE OR TREASURE?

Many of the shells I've collected are beautiful to me because of their imperfections. Some of the most special have the uniqueness of debris or growths on them. One small shell has a crescent of sand stuck hard to the outer surface. Embedded in the sand are tiny fragments of other shells. Another has a line of purple barnacles attached. Still another has a growth of coral on top which is much larger than the original shell. One of my favorites looks like a green frog. On the underside, part of a small shell is visible. I'm not sure what it is that has been sculpted onto it to form this image, but it amazes me.

These shells represent the garbage in our lives that not only hits us, but sticks to us. When we put ourselves into God's hands, he doesn't always remove what we think is garbage. Often, he takes it and with loving hands, sculpts it into something far more unique and beautiful than we could have imagined.

For our present troubles are small and won't last very long. Yet they produce for us a glory that vastly outweighs them and will last forever! So we don't look at the troubles we can see now; rather, we fix our gaze on things that cannot be seen. For the things we see now will soon be gone, but the things we cannot see will last forever. 2 Corinthians 4:17 (NLT)

MORNING'S HAZE

Gazing out the window that overlooked the ocean, I was amazed. In the early morning light there was just one solid colour before me. The sea and sky had blended seamlessly, with no distinction to mark where one ended and the other began. It was confusing but mesmerizing. Soon the sky began to brighten, the sea darkened and the horizon appeared in its rightful place once again.

This reminded me of times when life has seemed a blur. It had no clear definition, making it difficult to know up from down. At times like this I'm disoriented and not sure of my direction. Although it may seem like this will last forever, I know in my heart that it won't. In reality this is a reminder to me that I don't have the ability to handle every situation on my own. When I take my cares to Jesus I find that soon the Son of God will shine into my life, burning off the haze and bringing clarity to my focus once again.

For the Lord your God is living among you. He is a mighty savior. He will take delight in you with gladness. With his love, he will calm all your fears. He will rejoice over you with joyful songs. Zephaniah 3:17 (NLT)

PERSEVERANCE

"I would really like a picture of those shore birds," I said. "Not the tiny ones, but the others." My husband took the camera and set about getting close enough to get a good picture. These birds blended in quite well with their surroundings, so we knew it would be a challenge. Soon we spotted one that was just what I was looking for. Surprisingly it seemed to keep an even pace with his steps, always just a little too far ahead. A couple of times he was close enough, raised the camera, and just before the shutter clicked, the bird flew off. As if this wasn't bad enough, it made a sound like it was laughing at him! We had seen these birds take off in flight many times, but never with a sound like this.

A lesser man would have given up, at least for the time being. Not Brian. He persevered and eventually managed to get a few good pictures for me. That day my lesson came from my husband and not from nature. The easy thing to do would have been to give up saying that at least he tried. Instead he kept going until he achieved what he had set out to do.

If I can use this as my inspiration to keep moving toward my goal, not letting setbacks stop me, I will be able to reach so much more than I thought possible.

I have fought the good fight. I have completed the race. I have kept the faith. 2 Timothy 4:7 (GWT)

SEAWEED

We had arrived in the Mexican state of Yucatan, to a seaport town called Progreso. We were away from the cold Canadian winter but even though the temperatures were very warm, there were reminders that it was still winter here.

When the 'nortes' or north winds come, they send waves crashing to the shore, stirring up the sand beneath so the water is no longer crystal clear. Along with the sand and fragments of shells, they also toss seaweed onto the shore. The appearance is not pristine, but there is a rugged beauty in this natural state.

As we went for our much-loved walk along the beach we encountered clear areas before reaching others where we needed to climb over and through the spongy carpet of dry seaweed. At one time this seaweed served a valuable purpose, providing nourishment for the sea life. Now it was simply a hindrance to those on shore.

It may have slowed us down but didn't stop us from continuing our walk. There were still discoveries to be made further down the beach. We were rewarded with some unique shells, a friendly local coming out to greet us and the indescribable peace that is found in nature.

When others told us they no longer walked on the beach because of the seaweed, at first I felt sad for them. Then, I reflected on the times that I have been stopped in my tracks by things that were uncomfortable to cross through. Some, like the seaweed, were valuable in the past, but are no longer useful. By refusing to deal with the unpleasantness, the less than perfect conditions, I am forced to turn back instead of moving forward. Who knows what beauty and blessings I have missed by only taking the easy route? No more – I have caught a glimpse of what awaits me on the other side of the weeds, and know that it is something I want more of.

The Lord will be your confidence. He will keep your foot from getting caught. Proverbs 3:26 (GWT)

SAND BAGS

In coastal communities, sand bags are an important part of life. They are a necessary precaution. Day after day we walked past two men filling and tying sandbags. Not only is it hard work in the hot sun but they are very heavy to put into place. The men would look up, smile and wave as we walked past and then were back to work. They knew that these sandbags would help hold the waves back from their property.

As I looked at the sandbags I wondered what I am doing to shore up my life. Have I taken the time, put in the work, to ensure I will make it through the storms? When the waves of adversity hit, as they do to all of us at some point, will I be swept away?

The sandbags that will protect me are built of my faith in Jesus. He hasn't promised that there will be no more storms, but he has promised to walk with me as I go through them. He is my refuge and my strength, an ever present help in times of trouble. That is all the assurance that I need.

It is God who arms me with strength and keeps my way secure. Psalm 18:32 (NIV)

God is our refuge and strength, an ever-present help in trouble. Psalm 46:1 (NIV)

THICK OR THIN

When we are out walking along the beach, questions come to my mind that have no easy answers. One day it was "Why do you suppose some shells become thick and rough as they weather the tides, while others become thin and almost translucent?" After assuring my husband that I didn't expect him to have the answer, I started to ponder the question.

Maybe they were different types of shells. While this may be true in some cases, we had seen enough shells in the process of becoming smooth and translucent that I knew this wasn't the only answer.

Perhaps it has something to do with resistance. In order to fight the changes happening, I sometimes build up a thick protective layer around me. If, on the other hand, I don't resist, but accept these changes the result is different. When I realize that I need to find value in all things, my attitude helps to smooth the rough spots. In this way my life will take on a new beauty, one that shimmers and reflects the light to others.

This may not be the correct answer to my earlier question, but for now it is the one that I am going to go with!

He comforts us whenever we suffer. That is why whenever other people suffer, we are able to comfort them by using the same comfort we have received from God. 2 Corinthians 1:4 (GWT)

TIDES

Upon checking the tide schedule we knew that the water would be high that week. There would not be much change between low and high tide. We knew that this would cause a few challenges on our walk along the beach, but were not going to let that stop us.

When we came to a tricky spot, Brian showed me how to watch the waves so we would know the best time to make our crossing. Jokingly I said, "So I shouldn't just rush in, but wait for the right timing?" We looked at each other with the realization that this applied to so much more in life than this present situation.

In life I often rush into things without gathering enough information to see if the timing is right. When I decide that I want something, I want it now. One of the hardest lessons I have learned is that God's timing is not the same as mine. Sometimes, the waiting brings lessons of its own. Sometimes, by waiting, I am rewarded with something far greater than what I had originally wanted. God's timing is always perfect.

But as for me, I watch in hope for the Lord. I wait for God my Savior; my God will hear me. Micah 7:7 (NIV)

I say to myself, "The Lord is my portion; therefore I will wait for him. The Lord is good to those whose hope is in him, to the one who seeks him; it is good to wait quietly for the salvation of the Lord." Lamentations 3:24-26 (NIV)

WHERE TO BUILD

While on a walk I passed by a house in ruins, built on the sandy shore. As I looked at it I couldn't help but think of a song I learned as a child in Sunday School. The song talked about the wise man building his house upon the rock and the foolish man building his house upon the sand. I may not remember all of the words now, but I certainly remember the message of the song. The house on the rock stood firm, while the one on the sand collapsed. You see, the sand shifts, but the rock holds firm.

In my life, the rock is Jesus. He is the firm foundation I need in order to stand strong. When I anchor myself to him, I can survive the storms of life that hit me. I may be battered, but he holds me tight to ensure that I will make it through.

Looking at this house reminded me how thankful I am that my house is built on the rock, the firm foundation of Jesus.

"I will show you what he is like who comes to me and hears my words and puts them into practice. He is like a man building a house, who dug down deep and laid the foundation on rock. When a flood came, the torrent struck that house but could not shake it, because it was well built. But the one who hears my words and does not put them into practice is like a man who built a house on the ground without a foundation. The moment the torrent struck that house, it collapsed and its destruction was complete." Luke 6:47-49 NIV

WINDS OF CHANGE

We were in Mexico and the wind had changed direction. This day it was coming from the north. When the norte comes, it brings several days of cooler weather, sometimes accompanied by rain. As well as feeling the difference in the air, it can be seen by looking out at the water.

The sea is frothing with whitecaps that crash to the shore. More of its contents are stirred up and tossed onto the beach. This wildness only lasts a short time and soon we are returned to the warm gentle breezes of the south and to peaceful waters. Walking on the beach after a storm is filled with adventure as we discover new things that have been brought to shore.

The winds of change hit our lives with the same kind of force. One day we are walking with the sun on our faces and a gentle breeze at our backs. The next day we are assaulted by a cold wind hitting us and attempting to knock us down. Sometimes it hits us so hard that we don't know if we'll survive. It may not seem possible at the time, but one day we'll return to the sunshine and soft breezes.

The winds of change will hit all of us at some time. What I need to ask myself is, "What will I do when the wind changes direction in my life?" and "What will I do with the discoveries brought to light?"

If any of you lacks wisdom, he should ask God who gives generously to all without finding fault, and it will be given to him. But when he asks, he must believe and not doubt, because he who doubts is like a wave of the sea, blown and tossed by the wind. James 1:5 (NIV)

Inspirations While on the Road

REST AREA

Have you ever paid attention to the Rest Area signs when driving a distance? They are something that we tend to ignore until we need them. When a stop is needed we are on the lookout for these signs because we know that they will lead us to a safe place to pull off of the highway and take a break.

While I was on a road trip, I realized that there is more than one type of rest area. Some signs just said Rest Area and some said Partnership Rest Area. This got me to thinking of the times that I need to stop and rest. Sometimes I need to just take a break from everything and everyone and other times that rest needs to be taken with my partner. The rest refreshes us and prepares us to get back into the flow of life again.

In all the hustle and bustle of our busy lives it is more important than ever that we stop and take a rest. Trying to do everything can be very stressful. When you get overwhelmed with all that you need to do, stop and think of the Rest Area sign and either on your own, or with loved ones, take a detour off of the busy highway and rest awhile with Jesus. He wants to be our partner and give us the rest we desire as we spend time with Him. You'll be so glad you did.

But let all who take refuge in you be glad; let them ever sing for joy. Psalm 5:11(NIV)

UNDER CONSTRUCTION

I had just returned from a road trip with a couple of friends. This seemed to be the time of year that there was a lot of road construction going on. Some roads had barriers blocking off one lane while the road was being improved. Others were full of potholes that jarred the vehicle as we drove through them. One stretch of road had so many patches of fresh tar, that driving around them was like being on an obstacle course. A few times we travelled on gravel for several kilometers.

All of this reminded me of life. Our lives are constantly under construction. We're jarred by the unexpected potholes we encounter. Lots of times we have problems that stick to us like tar. We don't fully appreciate the smooth road of life until we have bumped along on the gravel for awhile. Just like driving on roads under construction, things may be tougher to navigate but we can do it if we slow down and consider the situation we are travelling through. God is working in us, reconstructing and repairing the damage that has been done. The process is not always pleasant, but it is necessary to enable us to travel the road that He has prepared for us.

And I am certain that God, who began the good work within you, will continue his work until it is finally finished on the day when Christ Jesus returns. Philippians 1:6 (NLT)

WEIGH STATIONS

Have you ever noticed the signs for highway scales or weigh stations? These are checkpoints along the highway to inspect the weight of large vehicles. The big trucks pull off and line up to get weighed. It is important to know how big a load they are carrying. The trucks will need to go through this process more than once on their long trips. This is to ensure that they haven't added to their loads and now weigh too much. More weight on the road per tire slowly breaks the road down, so this is for the safety of the road as well as the truck.

The more I think about it, the more I realize that weigh stations would be a good idea for me as well. As I travel the road of life, the load I carry can increase so gradually that I'm not even aware of it. The stress on me is not only difficult, but the effect on those around me can be less than pleasant as well. When I regularly check in with God, through prayer and reading the Bible, my load is weighed and I am given the opportunity to drop part or all of it. In this way my load will never be more than I can safely carry.

Therefore, since we are surrounded by such a huge crowd of witnesses to the life of faith, let us strip off every weight that slows us down, especially the sin that so easily trips us up. And let us run with endurance the race God has set before us. (Hebrews 12:1 NLT)

SHADOWS

While driving on a sunny morning I was amused by the shadow of our car. The angle of the sun had the shadow removed quite a bit from the car instead of appearing attached. The car looked to be short and squat, sitting on enormous tires. We had to laugh at the image of our "raised up" car.

Merriam-Webster dictionary defines shadow as: "A dark area or shape produced by a body coming between rays of light and a surface."

This got me to thinking about the shadows in my life. When I am in the shadows, things seem distorted, much like the image of our car did. I do not see a true picture of my life. There is no colour in the images I see, only darkness. What I need to remember is the darkness and distortion is not the reality. Something is temporarily blocking the sunshine to create these shadows. Too often, it is me. I read a quote from Ralph Waldo Emerson that said "Most of the shadows of life are caused by standing in our own sunshine." How true that is.

Shadows in our lives are only temporary. It may seem like a long wait sometimes, but the sunshine always reappears. Something I remind myself of when I am in the shadows is found in the 23rd Psalm. It says, "Though I walk through the valley of the shadow of death…" This tells me that I will not be left in that valley of shadow, but I must go through it to get to the other side. Whatever is causing the shadows in your life, keep walking through them and one day you will be in the sunshine again.

They spring up like flowers and wither away; like fleeting shadows, they do not endure. Job 14:2 (NIV)

HOPE

We had been driving through the mountains and were nearing a town called Hope. When I looked at the sign telling us how much farther before we would reach Hope, I wondered why my hope is often a distance away instead of being where I am now. Making our descent toward the town, we saw a "chain off" area where vehicles can pull over and remove the chains that are needed to get them safely through the steep mountain roads in winter conditions.

The significance of this combination of chains off before I reach Hope was not lost on me. When I am in situations in which I do not feel safe, I have been known to wrap chains around my heart for protection. At these times, hope seems so far away. It doesn't appear to get any closer as I journey along.

When I lay my concerns at the feet of Jesus, he releases the chains that have held me in bondage. I am free and realize that hope is now within me. I have found the true hope that will never leave me and that is the one found in Jesus.

May the God of hope fill you with all joy and peace as you trust in him, so that you may overflow with hope by the power of the Holy Spirit. Romans 15:13 (NIV)

Let us hold unswervingly to the hope we profess, for he who promised is faithful. Hebrews 10:23 (NIV)

LIFE IS A HIGHWAY – OR IS IT?

While on a road trip we were talking about life being a highway. In the song Life is a Highway the lyrics tell us that life is like a road that you travel on. We are also told that sometimes we have to bend and sometimes turn our backs to the wind. Basically, the song is telling us that we need to keep traveling on, through the tough times as well as the good times.

As we talked about this, the question was posed, "If life is truly a highway, where are the directional signs that help us navigate safely to our destination?" I'm certain that we have such signs; they are just far more subtle than those on the highway. Wouldn't it be nice to have written signs appear before us as we travel the road of life? That way there is less chance of missing them.

Imagine a sign that warns us we are going the wrong way. I can think of times in my life that a sign like this would have been of great benefit. How about ones letting us know when to slow down, or when there's a bump in the road ahead? It would also be helpful to have a sign warning us of slippery patches ahead. There are many more, but I'm sure you get the idea.

It sounds like a wonderful idea, but there would be drawbacks to all of these signs. If everything is always spelled out for us, when do we learn to trust God to guide us? I need to practice faith that he is in control and that I don't need to have all of the information in advance.

"Unless you people see signs and wonders," Jesus told him, "you will never believe." John 4:48 (NIV)

RECREATIONAL VEHICLES

We had driven past the RV Dealership many times before. One day, something caught my eye a little differently. The names of the different models were written in large letters on the sides of the units. I found it quite amusing to see 'Rushmore' on one of them. To me, the purpose of a recreational vehicle is to enable me to be in a place where I can relax, slow down and enjoy time outdoors. I'm not sure that I could achieve this in something that, every time I looked at it, reminded me to hurry, or rush more!

When I attempt to handle my life totally in my own strength I end up being in 'rush more' mode. On the other hand, when I pray and give control of my life to Jesus, my need to constantly do more and more becomes less important. There are still things that need to be accomplished but it is much easier to determine priorities. My timetable becomes more flexible. I have learned that all things happen in God's perfect timing.

I fall asleep in peace the moment I lie down because you alone, O Lord, enable me to live securely. Psalm 4:8 (GWT)

ARE WE THERE YET?

We were making the long drive from Calgary to Vancouver to visit friends and family. At one point I turned to Brian and said, "Are we there yet?" He smiled and said "Sure," knowing that we still had several hours ahead of us. We then joked about the fact that although we may not be "there" we were "here."

Despite the joking, this was a good reminder to me that I need to make the most of where I am right now. Sometimes I get so focused on getting to where I think I should be that I don't see what is surrounding me right now. There may be scenic routes that I miss by not paying attention. Not only do I miss out for myself, but opportunities to do things for others are surely lost as well.

Before I wake up in the morning, God has many wonderful things planned for my day. I need to start my day by praying and then trust God to lead me. When I do this, I remember that although I may not be where I thought I would be, I am exactly where I am supposed to be.

In the morning, Lord, you hear my voice; in the morning I lay my requests before you and wait expectantly. Psalm 5:3 (NIV)

DIGITAL SIGNS

I was driving on the highway when I saw a large digital sign that is often used to report road or traffic conditions. When there are no specific conditions that need to be reported, these signs often carry a public service type of message. This message usually flashes up in two parts and I've often wondered if it makes a difference which part of the message you read first. In this case it did. I saw "What's holding you back?" By the time the next part came up with a reminder about the importance of wearing seatbelts, my mind was already going in a completely different direction.

Instantly I thought about what had held me back in life. For the most part, I had done a very good job of holding myself back. Fears, self-doubts and trying to be what I thought others wanted me to be had kept me stuck and unable to move forward to where I needed to be. It was only when I allowed myself to dream and to let God guide those dreams that I had the confidence to move ahead.

I have a little plaque in my house that says, "Where God guides, He provides." When I follow in the way that God is guiding me, He provides so much more than I could ever have dreamt of. Once I can truly let him guide me, there is nothing holding me back.

Trust God from the bottom of your heart; don't try to figure out everything on your own. Listen for God's voice in everything you do, everywhere you go; he's the one who will keep you on track. Proverbs 3:5,6 (MSG)

CRUISE CONTROL

My husband picked up a rental car for a business trip he was taking. After searching everywhere for the cruise control, he finally came to the conclusion that this car was missing that option. It's something that is standard on most vehicles so this was a surprise. He had a lot of driving to do over the next few days and found the lack of cruise control more than an inconvenience. Not only was it difficult to maintain an even speed on long stretches of highway, his foot got very tired with no rest from the gas pedal.

Cruise control doesn't mean that the driver does not need to pay attention. You still have to steer and be aware of road conditions. What it does mean is that unless you hit the brake, your speed remains constant.

Sometimes I would like to put my life on cruise control. I still want control but I would prefer the ride to be smooth and consistent. Life, however, is not like that. If life was totally predictable it would be boring. Should I choose to take only the easy road I will miss the excitement of hairpin turns and the beauty of the high peaks. When I let Jesus take control of my life it is full of surprises. He has taken me to wonderful places that I would never have found on my own. Not only does he control the speed but the steering and direction are also taken care of for me. All I have to do is trust and I know I'm in for the ride of my life!

[The Lord says,] "I will instruct you. I will teach you the way that you should go. I will advise you as my eyes watch over you." Psalm 32:8 (GWT)

WAIT FOR THE DUST TO SETTLE

The phrase 'wait for the dust to settle' is one I've heard many times in my life. The meaning was to be patient until things calmed down. That, I understood.

One day that phrase had a whole new visual to give it effect. There are many dry dirt or gravel roads in the countryside. As I watched vehicles speed along them, I saw the tremendous amount of dust that was produced. The faster the vehicle travels, the more dust is produced.

If I race along behind, in this cloud of dust, my vision is impaired and the dust fills my lungs, making me uncomfortable. There's the option of waiting until the dust settles and ensuring my journey will be clearer and more pleasurable. It may appear to take longer, but as I have a more even pace, not having to slow down for the dust, the timing may not be all that different. There is also the added benefit of having a clear vision of where I'm going.

From another view-point, when I race selfishly along, what kind of dust am I producing for those that come behind me? Am I responsible for slowing down the progress of others? I need to be considerate of those who come behind as well as paying attention to those in front.

This is a life reminder for me. Whenever I see those dusty roads, I need to think 'when the dust settles' and check the pace of my life.

Be still before the Lord and wait patiently for him; do not fret when people succeed in their ways, when they carry out their wicked schemes. Psalm 37:7 (NIV)

Be patient, then, brothers and sisters, until the Lord's coming. See how the farmer waits for the land to yield its valuable crop, patiently waiting for the autumn and spring rains. You too, be patient and stand firm, because the Lord's coming is near. James 5:7,8 (NIV)

Inspirations From This and That

DONUTS

We decided to pick up donuts as a treat for our grandchildren. There were many different varieties so we made our choices carefully. The ones we chose had icing colours that we thought they would like. We also chose a chocolate one in case they needed another option. Our granddaughter chose the pink icing with sprinkles and was very happy with it. Our grandson chose the one with white icing and coloured stripes. His donut, however, was a disappointment. What none of us knew until he bit into it was that it had jelly inside.

Reflecting on this, I thought of all the choices I have had to make in life. Sometimes the sparkles have attracted me and influenced my decision. At times I have chosen what looks good on the surface, but it hasn't turned out to be what I thought it would. The plain version may have been better after all. I cannot always tell until I have committed to my choice. The surprise inside is sometimes a treat and other times a disappointment.

This was a good reminder for me that I don't have all of the information needed to make a proper decision on my own. I need to pray about things and then let God guide me. It is when I follow His plan that I know things will turn out alright.

A person may plan his own journey, but the Lord directs his steps. Proverbs 16:9 (GWT)

SOMETIMES YOU JUST NEED TO SHOW UP

Making a difference is something that many of us aspire to. In fact, several years ago, when asked what title I would choose for a book based on my life, I answered, "She Made a Difference." We think that we must do something big, something noteworthy, to make a difference. In actual fact, sometimes all we need to do is be present. This is something I have learned firsthand. The last few years I have been a mentor with Big Brothers Big Sisters. This is not their regular program, but instead is spending one hour a week, during the school day with a student. We don't do school work, just spend time together. It seems like such a simple thing. Other than getting her out of class for an hour, am I really doing something that impacts her life?

Usually we play card or board games. Occasionally we bake something. There is limited sharing but the relationship has become more familiar and now includes some laughter and teasing. She doesn't give me a lot of details of her life and I don't probe. Questions tend to shut her down. We'd been together for a year and a half and it still didn't feel to me like we had a great connection. My schedule was changing and it wasn't always possible to meet every week. Maybe it was better for her to have a new mentor, one that could not only be there every week, but could connect with her on a deeper level. I told the mentoring coordinator and the school counselor of my decision. When I told my mentee, the response was totally unexpected. She fought for me! She told the powers that be, that she would rather see me every other week that someone else every week. A bond had been built that was stronger than I had realized. The rules were bent to allow this match to continue.

A meeting with the coordinator a few months later let me know that my showing up, giving her my time, had indeed impacted this girl's life. I sat with tears running down my cheeks as I was told of ways that I had made a difference in her life not only for today, but to be carried into the future. It seemed like such a little thing, spending an hour together. Other than her birthday and Christmas, I brought no gifts. That's where my thinking was wrong. The gift I brought was the gift of me, of caring enough to be there and spend time with her. The gift that she has given me is showing me that it doesn't take grand gestures or huge sacrifices to make a difference. Sometime all you need to do is just show up.

Be devoted to one another in love. Honor one another above yourselves. Romans 12:10 (NIV)

Direct your children onto the right path, and when they are older, they will not leave it. Proverbs 22:6 (NLT)

MEDICINE

My granddaughter was prescribed antibiotics after being diagnosed with strep throat. Finding them unpleasant, she told her mom that she didn't like taking her medicine. Knowing the pills would make her feel better didn't make swallowing them any easier.

Thinking about this I realized how often I have fought accepting what was medicine for my life. The things that would help my physical and emotional health often seemed like bitter medicine when first introduced. The old saying about being a bitter pill to swallow comes to mind.

Just as I know that taking the unpleasant medicine is necessary to bring about healing, I also understand that challenges may come when I do what I must to achieve positive results in my life. Whatever I'm facing, there's comfort in knowing that Jesus, the Great Physician, has me in His loving care and will guide me through.

Wait with hope for the Lord. Be strong, and let your heart be courageous. Yes, wait with hope for the Lord. Psalm 27:14 (GWT)

"It is not the healthy who need a doctor, but the sick. I have not come to call the righteous, but sinners." Mark 2:17 (NIV)

DANCE RECITALS

We had the pleasure of attending a dance recital that our four and a half year old granddaughter was in. While there were also older, more accomplished dancers in the recital, it was the little ones who stole the show. They had such a joy about them and for the most part, seemed unconcerned if they were in rhythm with the music or each other. One little girl repeated the same move over and over as she smiled out into the audience. The fact that the others were not doing the same as her was something she didn't even notice!

These mistakes are what provide the most memorable moments. They also remind us that true joy comes from being loved by God, no matter how many mistakes we make. Our heavenly Father loves us unconditionally. His love is there when we move with the rhythm and when we get mixed up. He is there cheering us on, just like the loving parents watching the children in their recitals.

I need to remember to be more like a little child, not worried about my performance, just basking in the love of my Heavenly Father.

Our Father in heaven, hallowed be your name, your kingdom come, your will be done, on earth as it is in heaven. Matthew 6:9,10 (NIV)

one God and Father of all, who is over all and through all and in all. Ephesians 4:6 (NIV)

WHAT MATTERS MOST

There are many tragedies in the world today. Some are reported in the media while others hit much closer to home. A much loved teen losing a battle with cancer, senseless violence that claims lives that were far too short or a seemingly healthy adult being taken suddenly by a previously unknown illness. You know of many such stories. They are present in our lives and those of our loved ones.

Why then, do we still focus on things that don't matter in the grand scheme of things? Yes, everyday things still need to be taken care of, but not at the expense of relationships or making a difference in the world around us.

When we pass on, there won't be comments like, "She was a good person, too bad her house wasn't spotless." or, "He was a good father but should have spent more time at work." or even, "She was active in her community, what a shame she never lost that 20 pounds." What I want people saying about me was that I loved deeply and was committed to my family and friends. I want them to recognize that I did my best to not only see the positive, but to show it to others. It is important to me that I make a difference, that the world is a better place for my having been here. Most of all, I want others to know that I had a deep faith in God, one that not only carried me through but inspired others to also seek him.

None of this can be accomplished if I prefer to communicate through texts, or play computer games instead of sitting face to face with someone. What matters most is spending quality time with friends and family. Give lots of hugs, let people know you care about them. Live, laugh, love and thank God for every day he gives you.

For we are God's handiwork, created in Christ Jesus to do good works, which God prepared in advance for us to do. Ephesians 2:10 (NIV)

BIG ENOUGH?

We had three young granddaughters with us for the night. In the morning I was helping them put their tights on as we got dressed for church. When it was my turn to get ready and they looked at the pantyhose I was about to put on, I was told, "It's not big enough." Then, they watched in amazement as my hosiery stretched to fit. Since their tights were white and mine were skin coloured, it must have looked like my legs were still bare, and the girls stroked them occasionally, just to be sure!

My husband and I joked about this later and knew it would make a good story, but also wondered if there was a lesson here for us. With a little more thought, we realized that the lesson pointed us back to God. I can't see him and even though I know he's with me, sometimes I want something I can touch to make it real. Do I often treat God as 'not big enough' to handle the circumstances I am going through? Even though I give my concerns up to him, I know there are times when I think he just might need my help with them.

Jesus made the lame to walk and the blind to see. He is more than able to handle anything that comes my way. He loved me enough to die on a cross for me and then three days later, rose from the dead to guarantee my salvation. This is more than enough proof that he loves me and is always willing and able to take care of me. When I stop to really think about it, the only thing not big enough in this picture is my ability to get out of the way and let him work.

When you're in over your head, I'll be there with you. When you're in rough waters, you will not go down. When you're between a rock and a hard place, it won't be a dead end – Because I am God, your personal God, The Holy of Israel, your Savior. Isaiah 43:2,3 (MSG)

SURPRISE!

Have you ever planned and successfully pulled off a surprise for someone? My family did just that. We planned a surprise birthday party for my husband. We knew it had a good chance of being successful. The party was to be three weeks after his birthday so he shouldn't suspect a thing. Nevertheless, I found myself thinking about it constantly, especially in the few weeks preceding the party. With limited space, who would we invite? How could I contact people without him finding out? And, the biggest one of all, how would I get him there?

The goal in all of this was to honour a wonderful man by letting him know how much he was loved and appreciated. My concern was having to deceive him. I am not good at, nor do I want to be good at, lying to someone. The trick was to tell the truth in such a way that his interpretation would be slightly different from mine. Is that still lying? Something that was very apparent to me during this was that anything less than total honesty is stressful. I was constantly thinking about and monitoring my words. There were many things I wanted to say but couldn't.

The cause was a good one. The result was what we were hoping for. The surprise, however, was for more than the guest of honour. For me, I realized anew how lies and secrets affect our lives. My thoughts were so focused on how to achieve the end goal without giving away the secret that I was unable to focus on other things. My waking thoughts were consumed with this. When I am being totally honest I don't have to worry about keeping my story straight. I can focus on the task at hand instead of how I'm going to explain things. It seems that this surprise had a double purpose. The first was to honour a loved one. The second was a powerful reminder that it's always better to be truthful.

Then you will know the truth, and the truth will set you free. John 8:32 (NIV)

The one whose walk is blameless, who does what is righteous, who speaks the truth from their heart; Psalms 15:2 (NIV)

THANKSGIVING

Thanksgiving is a day set aside for us to give thanks, so important that it is a statutory holiday in Canada and the United States. Many of us gather with loved ones to enjoy a turkey dinner. Some may share what they are thankful for.

I know that when I sit down to Thanksgiving dinner with family, the bounty of food before us will only be a small part of what I am thankful for. I am thankful for a wonderful husband who is a gift not only to me and to our family, but also to those fortunate enough to know him. I am also thankful for our children and their spouses and the time we enjoy spending together. The joyful sounds of our grandchildren remind me how blessed we are to live close enough to be able to play a significant role in their lives.

All of us have so much to be thankful for. Taking time to stop and do this on a daily basis can change your life. It did mine. For over ten years now I have been keeping a gratitude journal. Every night I write down five things that I was grateful for that day. Some days it is basic things like a roof over my head and food to eat. Others it is a smile from a stranger, a phone call from a friend or the beauty of nature. One of my favourites is the excited squeal of grandchildren as they run and throw themselves into my arms. There is much to be thankful for, and now I look for these things every day. This allows me to focus on all the good things that God continuously provides. No matter what my day may bring, I am confident that God is watching over me.

Enter his gates with thanksgiving and his courts with praise; give thanks to him and praise his name. For the Lord is good and his love endures forever; his faithfulness continues through all generations. Psalm 100:4,5 (NIV)

Rejoice always, pray continually, give thanks in all circumstances; for this is God's will for you in Christ Jesus. 1 Thessalonians 5:16-18 (NIV)

TO OR WITH?

Someone mentioned to me that they had been talking with a mutual friend. As I reflected on this later, I realized that talking to and talking with are not the same thing. When talking 'to' someone, I am putting the emphasis on me. It's me doing the talking. If I'm talking 'with' someone, it is a shared conversation and both of us have an active part in it. Both of us talk and both listen.

It saddens me to think about how many times I've been involved in the 'talking to' scenario. I've played both roles and clearly remember being talked 'to', and how that felt. Knowing that I've also done the talking 'to' is not a comfortable feeling. Now that this is so clear in my mind I can stop myself when I start talking 'to' and change it to talking 'with'.

One of the areas that I need to practice this is in my communication with God. Too often I've talked to Him about my concerns, asked for help or advice, and then moved on with my day without stopping to listen for His response. He does hear me and have answers for me but I'll only know what He's saying if I concentrate on the other important part of communication – the listening.

"Ask and it will be given to you; seek and you will find; knock and the door will be opened to you. For everyone who asks receives; the one who seeks finds; and to the one who knocks, the door will be opened. Matthew 7:7,8 (NIV)

SCARS

I have a scar on one of my fingers. It came from an incident when I was an awkward pre-teen and fell while roller skating. My hand hit the ground while my feet were still moving and I skated over my finger. It was very embarrassing at the time, but now it just makes for a good story! Rarely do I even notice this scar now, and when I do, I can smile and think of how my life has progressed since that gangly awkward stage.

There have been many scars in my life through the years. Some are visible to the eye and others are held deep within. A scar comes from a wound. All wounds eventually heal over, but one that has been properly cleansed and treated will cause fewer problems in the future than one that is left to fester.

I have had the privilege of working with some people who were brave enough to examine their scars, open up the old wounds and air them out to heal the poison that still caused them pain. It was not a comfortable process, but the true healing could not begin until this was done.

You see, they had learned the same lesson that I did. My scars do not define me. They serve to remind me of where I have been. They are not who I am now. When I let Jesus heal my wounds, the scars no longer need to be hidden. He cleanses them and removes the pain. Now I can look at my scars, be thankful for the lessons that come with them and realize how much I have grown since they were first formed.

He heals the brokenhearted and binds up their wounds. Psalm 147:3 (NIV)

CONTAGIOUS

As we enter cold and flu season we are warned to be diligent about washing our hands and using hand sanitizer. The goal is to avoid the contagious germs that seem to be infecting so many people.

Physical ailments aren't the only things that are contagious. After reading an article about attitudes, I realized that my attitude is also contagious to those I come in contact with. If I'm miserable, people will avoid me so they won't 'catch' my bad mood. When I am happy, positive and encouraging, people are glad to be around me. This is when they want to 'catch' what I have. When my positive attitude is 'caught' by another, that person tends to pass it on to someone else and it spreads. I actually have the potential to start an epidemic of happiness.

The question I need to ask myself is this, "If attitudes are contagious, is mine worth catching?"

A person's anxiety will weigh him down, but an encouraging word makes him joyful. Proverbs 12:25 (GWT)

To be made new in the attitude of your minds; Ephesians 4:23 (NIV)

ARCHERY

My daughter and her family have discovered that they enjoy archery. They made a visit to a facility where they could try this sport and liked it enough that they plan to return. I have been invited to join them next time but have mixed feelings about going.

Several years ago, I was at a weekend retreat where archery was offered. Despite some instruction, I couldn't get the arrow to do more than drop at my feet. Looking back on this, I wonder if I just didn't pull the arrow back enough before letting it go. You see, an arrow cannot shoot forward unless it is pulled back first.

This may also be something that I need to remember in life. When I feel like I'm being pushed backward with difficulties, I need to remember the arrow. God will not let me be stretched backward to the breaking point. He has something great in mind for me and I need to trust that he is preparing me for it even in the midst of my difficulties. Maybe I'm getting ready to be launched forward into something wonderful.

Wait for the Lord; be strong and take heart and wait for the Lord.
Psalm 27:14 (NIV)

CELEBRATIONS

In life we celebrate birthdays, anniversaries, graduations and other great achievements, but how many of us take the time to celebrate other things or at other times?

I watched a short video of a young couple with a very sick baby. Every day they celebrated the life and achievements of that child. They could have been angry and depressed, but chose instead to celebrate what they had, on a daily basis.

This is an extreme example but got me to thinking about the celebrations in my life. What if I set small goals and celebrated reaching each one of them, rather than waiting for the big goal to be accomplished. How much richer would my life be if I celebrated friends and family just because I love and appreciate them? What a joyous atmosphere I would create. A benefit of this would also be the residual effect. When I celebrate, I create positive feelings that make me want to do better so I can celebrate and experience these feelings again.

Celebrations not only feel good to us, they are also a way to thank God for all that he has given us. It is biblical to celebrate. So, what's stopping you? Get out there and celebrate your life and those that are a part of it. Today is that special occasion you've been waiting for.

They celebrate your abundant goodness and joyfully sing of your righteousness. Psalm 145:7 (NIV)

David and the whole company of Israel were in the parade, singing at the top of their lungs and playing mandolins, harps, tambourines, castanets, and cymbals. 2 Samuel 6:5 (MSG)

A LESSON

I was spending an hour during the school day with a 13 year old girl. We regularly meet as part of a mentoring program where the idea is just to spend time together to build a supportive relationship.

Upon spotting a crib board on the games shelf she was very excited as this was a game she had just learned a few days earlier. Unfortunately, not only were the pegs missing but there was also no deck of cards. I told her we would have to do something else for now. I would bring a crib board and cards from home the next time we met. She looked at me and said, "I don't give up that easily." The creative idea she came up with for pegs was to use staples. They sank too deep into the holes, so one end was straightened to give us something that we could grip. Then she went to the school counselor to ask for a deck of cards that we could use. Having everything we needed, happily she said, "See, I told you I don't give up easily." After saying that I appreciated that about her, we carried on, enjoying playing this game that she had just learned.

As our hour drew to a close and we packed away the game, she looked at me very seriously, saying, "I told you I didn't give up easily. There's a life lesson for you." She was right. As I drove away from the school, I reflected on how my life lessons come to me in completely unexpected ways.

As this book draws to a close, I know that there are still many lessons in store for me. God is continually inspiring me through the everyday things of life. As long as I slow down and pay attention, the lessons are never ending. They are meant to be shared with others and by doing this; I am living the life I was created for. Thank you for joining me on this journey.

If any of you lacks wisdom, you should ask God, who gives generously to all without finding fault, and it will be given to you. James 1:5 (NIV)

Printed in Canada